DOVER · THRIFT · EDITIONS

The Wisdom of the Talmud

Edited by

MADISON C. PETERS

DOVER PUBLICATIONS, INC.
Mineola, New York

DOVER THRIFT EDITIONS

GENERAL EDITOR: PAUL NEGRI
EDITOR OF THIS VOLUME: JOSLYN T. PINE

Published in Canada by General Publishing Company, Ltd., 30 Lesmill Road, Don Mills, Toronto, Ontario.

Bibliographical Note

This Dover edition, first published in 2001, contains selections from the work originally published in 1912 by the Bloch Publishing Company, New York, under the title *Wit and Wisdom of the Talmud*. And only the most relevant portion of Rabbi Mendes' Introduction to the original work has been included here.

Library of Congress Cataloging-in-Publication Data

Talmud. English. Selections.
The wisdom of the Talmud / edited by Madison C. Peters.
p. cm. — (Dover thrift editions)
"This Dover ed. . . . contains selections from the work originally published in 1912 by Bloch Publishing . . . under the title Wit and Wisdom of the Talmud"—CIP galley.
ISBN 0-486-41597-X (pbk.)
1. Peters, Madison Clinton, 1859–1918. II. Title.

BM499.5.E5 P48 2001
296.1'250521—dc21

00-069450

Manufactured in the United States of America
Dover Publications, Inc., 31 East 2nd Street, Mineola, N.Y. 11501

Introduction

THE TORAH (or law) was given A.M.* 2448. From the following forty years of the desert-life down to the present day, countless rulings, precedents, etc., have accumulated. Some are indicated in various passages in the Bible, e.g., ceremonies or rules observed in mourning, or have come to us by tradition.

Rabbi Judah Hanassi, surnamed the Holy, collected all attainable and published them in what we call the Mishna, A.M. 3980.

The Mishna contains six sections or Sedarim. Each section or Seder contains Massechtoth or treatises, as follows:

Section I: Seeds.—After a chapter devoted to the benedictions, it treats of tithes, first fruits, sacrifices, and gifts due from the produce of the land to the priests, the Levites, and the poor; of the cessation of agricultural labor during the Sabbatic year; and of the prohibited mixtures in seeds and in grafting.—In all eleven treatises.

Section II: Feasts.—Of the Sabbath and Sabbath rest, of feasts and fasts: Passover, Tabernacles, New Year, the Day of Atonement, and the Fasts; of work forbidden, ceremonies to be observed, and sacrifices to be brought on those days.—Twelve treatises.

Section III: Women.—The legislation concerning marriage, divorce, the levirate marriage, and adultery; vows and the regulations for the Nazirite.—Seven treatises.

Section IV: Fines.—Civil legislation, besides a tractate on idolatry, and one called *Aboth*, consisting of a collection of the ethical sentences of the Rabbis. This section treats of commercial transactions, purchases, sales, mortgages, prescriptions, etc.; of legal procedure, of the organization of tribunals, of witnesses, oaths, etc.—Ten treatises.

*A.M. = *anno mundi*] Literally, "in the year of the world," dating from the Creation in Jewish chronology, based on rabbinic calculations.

Section V: Sacred Things.—The legislation concerning sacrifices, the first-born, clean and unclean animals; the description of Herod's Temple.—Eleven treatises.

Section VI: Purifications.—Laws concerning Levitical cleanness and uncleanness; clean and unclean persons and things, objects capable of becoming unclean by contact. Purifications.—Twelve treatises.

Many decisions not included by Rabbi Jehudah, because not considered by him sufficiently authoritative, or because they were merely repetitions, were collected later under the name of Boraithoth in a work called the Tosiphtha, or Addition (Supplement), by Rabbis Hiya and Oshaya of Babylon. Yet other Boraithoth are to be found in the Gemara.

The Gemara is a comment on the Mishna, just as the Mishna is a comment on the Torah or Law. One Gemara, the work of the Palestine schools, inaccurately but generally called the Jerusalem Talmud, was edited in Tiberias about 380 C.E. The other, much larger, better known and constituting what is meant when the word "Talmud" is used, is the work of the Babylonian schools, and was edited by Rabbi Ashi and his disciple, Rabbi José, about 500 C.E. This is usually published with the commentary of the celebrated Rashi, and with comments called Tosephoth.

The Rabbis identified with the Mishna are called Tanaim, or teachers; those of the Gemara are called Amoraim, or speakers, and the latter commentators are called Seburaim, or opinionists. Imagine the debates, evidence or testimony, assertions, opinions, pro and con, identified with process of Law that continue through centuries. How much extraneous matter must naturally be met with! Imagine the debates, evidence, assertions, opinions, etc., pro and con, identified with processes of Law of only one year, of only one court, of only one modern city. How much information will be incidentally stated! It is not surprising, therefore, that we find incidentally stated in the Talmud much that may seem to have nothing to do with the case in point, but which is incidentally of value to a future student of men and manners, of value to historian, antiquarian, ethnologist, scientist, of value to preacher, lawyer, physician or other scientists, and of value to artisan, housewife, humorist and philosopher.

RABBI H. PEREIRA MENDES

Contents

ACTIONS

Actions speak louder than words.

✡

Judge a man by his deeds, not by his words.

✡

All the other rivers said to the Euphrates: "Why is the current of thy water not heard at a distance?" The Euphrates replied: "My deeds testify for me. Anything sown by men at my shores will be in full bloom within thirty days." The rivers then addressed the Tigris: "Why is the current of thy waters heard at a distance?" "I must direct the attention of the people to me by my tumultuous rapidity," the Tigris replied.

The moral: The less the merits of a person are, the more he will feel urged to proclaim them to the public.

✡

The forest trees once asked the fruit trees: "Why is the rustling of your leaves not heard in the distance?" The fruit trees replied: "We can dispense with the rustling to manifest our presence, our fruits testify for us." The fruit trees then inquired of the forest trees: "Why do your leaves rustle almost continually?" "We are forced to call the attention of man to our existence."

ADVERSITY

Adversity is the true school of the mind.

✡

When the ox is down, many are the butchers.

ADVICE

Not as thou sayest, but as thy fellows say.

✡

Too many captains sink the ship.

✡

Hear sixty advisers, but be guided by your own conviction.

✡

The action of a fool cannot serve as a precedent.

✡

Poor servants ask advice after a thing has happened.

✡

A thing to which a fool does not consent, know as the right thing.

AGE

None may be called venerable save the wise.

✡

Happy is the old age that atones for the follies of youth; but happier still the youth for which old age needs not to blush.

✡

An old man is a trouble in the house; an old woman is a treasure in the house.

ANCESTRY

He who has no inner nobleness has nothing, even if he be of noble birth.

ANGER

Anger profiteth nobody.

✡

Avoid anger and thou wilt not sin.

✡

Anger showeth the character of a man.

✡

To accept excuse shows a good disposition.

✡

The beginning of anger is madness, the end penitence.

✡

He who gives way to his wrath makes desolate his house.

✡

When the wise is angry, he is wise no longer.

✡

A man may be known by three things: by his conduct in money matters, his behavior at the table and his demeanor when angry.

✡

Be not easily moved to anger.

✡

To him who curbs his wrath, his sins will be forgiven.

✡

He who is slow to anger and easily pacified is truly pious and virtuous.

APPEARANCES

Two pieces of coin in one bag make more noise than a hundred.

Look not at the cask, but at what is in it. A new cask may contain old wine, and an old one may be altogether empty.

✡

Where the sages bid us beware for the sake of outward appearances, they mean us to regard even our innermost chamber as a marketplace.

ARROGANCE

Arrogance is a kingdom without a crown.

ASSOCIATES

Ever associate with the good.

✡

From vagrants chit-chat, from rags vermin.

✡

If thy associates be insane, be thou sensible.

✡

We may say to the bee, neither thy honey nor thy sting.

✡

Birds of a feather flock together; and so with men—like to like.

✡

Associate not with the wicked man, even if thou canst learn from him.

✡

A man without a fitting companion is like the left hand without the right.

✡

Not without reason goes the crow to the raven, but because it is of its kind.

If you touch pitch, it will stick to your fingers; even so, if you associate with evil companions, you will acquire their vices.

✡

It is beautiful and rejoicing to see grapes on the vine; it is ugly and repugnant to see grapes on a thorn-bush.

✡

When the iron was created the trees commenced to tremble. The iron, however, said to them: "What are you trembling at? If none of your wood will join me, I will remain harmless."

✡

Every beast associates with its kind, but man only with his equal. What can combine wolf with the sheep? So is the impious with the poor. Would the hyena associate with the dog? So the wealthy with the poor. The wild ass is torn to pieces by the lion, so the poor becomes the prey of the rich.

✡

When the flood came over the earth, and everything was threatened with destruction, and every kind of beast in pairs came to Noah, the Lie, too, asked admittance into the ark. Noah, however, refused. "Only pairs may enter here," he said. The Lie went in search of a companion, and at last met Vice, whom it invited to go to the ark. "I am willing to keep company with thee, if thou wilt promise to give me all thy earnings," said Vice. The Lie agreed, and they were both admitted into the ark. After they left the ark the Lie regretted her agreement, and wished to dissolve partnership with Vice; but it was too late, and thus it is current, that "what Lie earneth, Vice consumeth."

BRIBERY

A judge that takes a bribe, even if he be otherwise perfectly righteous, will not depart from the world before he has become demented.

BUSINESS

He laid his money on the horns of a deer.

Attend no auctions if thou hast no money.

✡

Keep partners with him whom the hour favors.

✡

If thy business does not prosper in one town try another.

✡

He who looks daily after his field finds a corn.

CARE

Let not your heart with cares be filled, for care has many a victim killed.

✡

Do not worry thyself with the trouble of to-morrow; perhaps thou wilt have no to-morrow, and why shouldst thou trouble thyself about a world that is not thine?

CHARACTER

Three names are given to a man: one by his parents, another by the world, and the third by his works—the one which is written in the immortal book of his fate. Which of these three names is the best? Solomon teaches us, when he says: "A good name is better than the sweetest oil."

✡

As a tree is known by its fruit, so man by his works.

✡

There are three crowns: that of the Law, the priesthood, and royalty; but the crown of a good name is loftier than all these.

✡

The righteous man is a pillar upon which all the world rests.

CHARITY

Charity is the salt of riches.

✡

Charity is the greatest virtue.

✡

Charity is more than sacrifices.

✡

Good deeds are better than creeds.

✡

He who gives charity in secret is greater than Moses.

✡

Even he who lives upon charity should practise benevolence.

✡

It is better to lend than to give. To give employment is better than either.

✡

The practice of beneficence will assure the maintenance of one's possessions.

✡

Our kindly deeds and our generous gifts go to heaven as messengers, and plead for us before our heavenly Father.

✡

He who turns away from the works of love and charity, turns away from God.

✡

The merit of charitable works is in proportion to the grace with which they are practiced.

✡

The noblest of all charities is in enabling the poor to earn a livelihood.

Charity is more valuable than sacrifices, and alone equals the exercise of all religious forms.

✡

As a garment is made up of single threads, so every single gift aids in building the great work of charity.

✡

It is our duty to relieve the poor and the needy, to visit the sick and bury the dead without distinction of race or creed.

✡

Whosoever engages in the study of the Law, and does not practise benevolence, is to be compared to a man who has no God.

✡

Spending alms and practising benevolence exceed in importance all the other laws of the Torah.

✡

The house that does not open to the poor will open to the physician.

✡

He gives little who gives with a frown. He gives much who gives little with a smile.

✡

The world stands on three things: on Law, Labor, and Benevolence.

✡

He who performs a single good action gains for himself an Advocate, and he who commits a single sin procures for himself an Accuser.

✡

Iron breaks stone; fire melts iron; water extinguishes fire; the clouds consume water; the storm dispels clouds; man withstands the storm; fear conquers man; wine banishes fear; sleep overcomes wine, and death is the master of sleep; but "Charity," says Solomon, "saves from death."

✡

Four dispositions are found among those who bestow charity. There is he who is willing to give, but does not wish others to give: he has an envious eye towards others. There is he who wishes others to give, but who will not give himself: he has an evil eye towards himself. He who is willing to give and wishes others to give also, is a pious man. He who neither gives himself nor wishes others to give, is a wicked man.

✡

Blessed is he who gives from his substance to the poor; twice blessed he who accompanies his gift with kind, comforting words.

✡

Almsgiving is practised by means of money, but charity also by personal services and by words of advice, sympathy, and encouragement. Almsgiving is a duty towards the poor only, but charity towards the rich as well as the poor, nay, even towards the dead (by taking care of their decent burial).

✡

Charitable people silence the complaints of the poor. God says to these pious ones: "By your liberality you reconcile the poor man with Myself; you make peace between us."

✡

He who hesitates in the practice of charity commits a sin. This is proven in the life of Nachum of Gamzoo, so called because whatever occurred to him, he was in the habit of saying: "This, too, is for the best." . . . In his old age he became blind; both of his hands and both of his feet were amputated, and the trunk of his body was covered with many sores. His scholars said to him: "If thou art a righteous man, why art thou so sorely afflicted?" "All this," he answered, "I brought upon myself. Once I was travelling to my father-in-law, and I had with me thirty asses laden with provisions and all manner of precious articles. A man by the wayside called to me: 'Oh, Rabbi, assist me.' I told him to wait until I had unloaded my asses. When I had removed the burdens from my beasts, and went to him, I found to my sorrow that he had fallen and expired. I threw myself upon his body and wept bitterly. 'Let these eyes, which had no pity on thee, be blind,' I said; 'these hands, that delayed to assist thee, let them be cut off, and also these feet, which did not run to aid thee.' And yet I was not satisfied until I had prayed that my whole body be stricken with sores."

✡

One day the Roman Governor, T. Annius Rufus, asked Rabbi Akiba: "If your God loves the poor among the Hebrews, why does He not support them?" "Because God desires to give the rich an opportunity of doing good," was the Rabbi's reply. "How do you know," Rufus rejoined, "that this virtue of charity pleases God, since no master can be pleased, if a person aids a slave, whom he has seen fit to deprive of food and clothing?" "Even so," said Akiba; "but if the king, for some offence, had deprived his son of food and drink, and a person had prevented the prince from dying of hunger, would the king be wroth with that person? Certainly not, neither will God be displeased with those who dispense charity to His children, even to the fallen and the sinful."

CLEANLINESS

Poverty comes from God, but not dirt.

COMMERCE

Credit and mutual trust should be the foundation of commercial intercourse.

CONCEIT

Ignorance and conceit go hand in hand.

✡

Take out the beam from thine eye.

✡

First correct thyself, then correct others.

CONSISTENCY

There are some who preach beautifully, but practise not their beautiful doctrine.

The learned man should judge himself according to his own teaching, and not do anything that he has forbidden others to do.

✡

Beautiful are the admonitions of those whose lives accord with their teachings.

CONTENTMENT

Little is much, if the heart be but turned toward heaven.

✡

Who is rich? He who is satisfied with his lot.

✡

The camel wanted to have horns, and they took away his ears.

✡

One bird tied is better than a hundred flying.

✡

Drink not from one cup with thine eye fastened on another.

✡

The egg of to-day is better than the hen of to-morrow.

✡

A small quantity in the house is better than much at a distance.

✡

Grasp a little and you may secure it; grasp too much and you will lose everything.

✡

Better eat onions all thy life than dine upon geese and chickens once and then long in vain for more ever after.

✡

He that hires one garden will eat birds; he that hires many gardens, the birds will eat him.

Crave not after the table of kings: for thy table is greater than their table, and thy crown is greater than their crown; and the Master who employs thee is faithful to pay the reward of thy labor.

CONTRITION

One inward contrition in the heart of man is better than many flagellations.

CORDIALITY

Be in the habit of receiving every man with a pleasant countenance.

COSMETICS

Cold water, morning and evening, is better than all the cosmetics.

COVETOUSNESS

The question is asked, "Why is man born with hands clinched, but has his hands wide open in death?" And the answer is: On entering the world man desires to grasp everything, but when leaving it he takes nothing away.

Even as a fox who saw a fine vineyard, and lusted after its grapes, but being too fat to get through the only opening there was, he fasted three days. He then got in; but, having fed, he could not get out until he had fasted three days more. "Naked man enters the world, and naked does he leave."

CRUELTY TO ANIMALS

Do not put a greater burden upon thy beast than it can bear.

To have compassion upon animals is one of the laws of Moses.

✡

He who has no mercy upon animals shall himself suffer pain.

✡

A man should not buy cattle or poultry without having first bought food for them.

DEATH

Death is the haven of life, and old age the ship which enters the port.

✡

Do not speak ill of the departed, but remember that his soul still lives, though the body is dead.

✡

It is our duty to comply with the last wishes of a dying person.

DEBT

Go to sleep without supper, but rise without debt.

DECEIT

He who deceives his neighbor would also deceive his God.

✡

Under no consideration lead men astray.

There is no greater evil-doer than he who takes away the earnings of the poor.

✡

A lie has not a leg to stand upon.

DIGNITY

Dignity does not consist in a silk dress.

DISCORD

One loose cord loosens many.

DISCRETION

Thy friend has a friend, and thy friend's friend has a friend; be discreet.

DRESS

In the town where one lives the name will do; outside of it the dress must do.

✡

The learned man whose garment is soiled is undeserving of honor.

ECONOMY

Live within your means; spend more on your clothing and most on your home.

ENVY

An envious man frowns when his neighbor rejoices.

ERROR

Error soon loses itself.

EXAMPLE

Precept with example produces example.

✡

Two dry logs and one wet; the dry ones kindle the wet.

✡

Let every man watch his own doings that he may be an example to his fellow man through life.

EXPERIENCE

Experience is the mirror of the mind.

FAME

He who seeks fame often loses it.

FASTING

No one is permitted to afflict himself by unnecessary fasting.

FAULT-FINDERS

Man sees all the faults but his own.

✡

Do not blame in others your own faults.

He who seeks for a faultless brother will have to remain brotherless.

✡

He who sees his own faults is too much occupied to see the faults of others.

✡

He who blames others is full of blame himself; and the fault he sees in others may be seen in himself.

FELLOW MAN

He who raises a hand against a fellow man, even if he injure him not, is called wicked.

✡

He who shames a fellow man in public is a murderer.

FLATTERY

Let not your lips speak that which is not in your heart.

✡

Love those who reprove thee, and hate those who flatter thee; for reproof may lead thee to eternal life, flattery to destruction.

FOOLS

Do not live near a pious fool.

✡

An ass tied to the sun—(A fool in a high station).

The pious fool, the hypocrite, and the flagellating Pharisee* are destroyers of human society.

✡

Be not the friend of one who wears the cloak of a saint to cover the moral deformities of a knave.

✡

If thy friends agree in calling thee an ass, go and get a halter around thee.

✡

Rather be thou called a fool all thy days than walk one hour before the All-Seeing Eye in evil ways.

FORGIVENESS

It is sinful to hate, but noble to pardon.

✡

He who wishes to be forgiven must forgive.

FRAUDS

He who pretends to be halt or blind in order to appeal to popular sympathy, will be afflicted with these infirmities sooner or later.

FRIENDSHIP

Friendship or death.

✡

An old friend do not forsake.

---

*Pharisee] A member of an ancient Jewish group which was noted for the strict and formal observance of both the oral and written law.

Ascend a step in choosing a friend.

✡

To have no faithful friends is worse than death.

✡

If thy friend is honey, do not lick him up altogether.

✡

Thy own deeds make thy friends or thy enemies.

✡

One enemy is one too many, a thousand friends are none too many.

✡

Do not blame thy friend for shortcomings which thou hast thyself.

✡

There are many friends at the door of the store, but there are none at the door of misery.

✡

The dog follows thee, but his attachment is to the crumb which he expects of thee.

✡

New things are the best things; old friends are the best friends.

✡

He who asks more of a friend than he can bestow, deserves to be refused.

✡

A man without friends is like the left hand without the right.

✡

Be humble to thy superior, affable to thy inferior, meet every man with friendliness.

✡

At the gate of abundance there are many brothers and friends; at the gate of misery there is neither brother nor friend.

GOD—HOLY LAW

Know that thou art always in God's Presence.

✡

Reverence of God is the basis of morality.

✡

We cannot comprehend either the prosperity or the sufferings of the righteous.

✡

From beginning to end God's law teaches kindness.

✡

Whatever God does is done for our good.

GOD'S PRESENCE

The consciousness of God's presence is the first principle of religion.

GOOD

Cling steadfastly to that which is good.

✡

There are three who are especially beloved by God: he who is forbearing, he who is temperate, and he who is courteous.

GRATITUDE

Men should thank God alike for evil and for good.

GREATNESS

How may a man obtain greatness? By fidelity, truth, and lofty thoughts.

GUILT

He who denies his guilt doubles his guilt.

✡

If any blame be attached to thee, be the first to declare it.

✡

He through whose agency another has been falsely punished stands outside of heaven's gates.

HABIT

Habit strips sin of its enormity.

✡

Habit becomes natural.

HOME LIFE

Duties Between Husbands and Wives

A man's home means his wife.

✡

Who is rich? He who has a good wife.

✡

An unkind wife is a mental affliction.

✡

From his first love man derives true wedded bliss.

Honor your wife that you may become rich.

✡

He who has no wife is esteemed as dead.

✡

He who divorces his wife is hated before God.

✡

Love your wife like yourself; honor her more than yourself.

✡

When the wife of a man's youth dies, the altar of the Lord is in mourning.

✡

A true wife makes the home a holy place.

✡

As soon as a man marries his sins decrease.

✡

He who lives without a wife is no perfect man.

✡

A man should be careful not to afflict his wife, for God counts her tears.

✡

He who marries for money, his children shall be a curse to him.

✡

Love your wife truly and faithfully, and do not compel her to hard work.

✡

If thy wife is small, bend down to take her counsel.

✡

Let a man be careful to honor his wife, for he owes to her alone all the blessings of his house.

Let youth and old age not be joined in marriage, lest the purity and peace of domestic life be disturbed.

✡

A man's wife has scarcely breathed her last when another is waiting to take her place.

✡

All the blessings of a household come through the wife, therefore should her husband honor her.

✡

First build a house and plant a vineyard (i.e., provide for the means of the household), and then take a wife.

✡

If in anger the one hand remove thy wife or thy child, let the other hand again bring them back to thy heart.

✡

All ailings, only not the ailing of heart; all evils, but not an evil wife.

✡

It is as difficult to effect suitable matrimonial matches as it was to divide the Red Sea.

✡

To be unmarried is to live without joy, without blessing, without kindness, without religion, and without peace.

✡

A handsome dwelling, a pretty wife, and beautiful furniture, exert a cheering influence upon a man's spirits.

✡

The husband should always endeavor to provide bread for his house, for quarrel begins mostly on account of improvidence.

✡

The majority of children resemble their maternal uncles; hence the choice of a wife should be determined by the character of her brothers.

He who loves his wife as his own self, and honors her more than himself, and he who educates his children in the right way, to him applies the Divine promise, "Thou shalt know that there is peace in thy tent."

✡

From the age of twenty, if a man remain in a state of celibacy, he lives in constant transgression. Up to that age the Holy One waits for him to enter the state of matrimony, and woe to his bones if he does not marry then!

✡

He who sees his wife die before him has, as it were, been present at the destruction of the Temple, and around him the world grows dark. It is woman alone through whom God's blessings are vouchsafed to a house. She teaches the children, speeds the husband to the house of worship and instruction, welcomes him when he returns, keeps the house godly and pure; and God's blessings rest upon all these things.

Duties Between Parents and Children

The daughter is as the mother was.

✡

When the calf kicks, 'tis time to thrash the cow.

✡

What the child says out of doors he has learnt in doors.

✡

The daughter's doings have been the mother's acts.

✡

Do not confine your children to your own learning, for they were born in another time.

✡

Where the children honor their parents, there God dwells, there He is honored.

✡

Parental love should be impartial; one child must not be preferred to the other.

The honor and reverence due to parents are equal to the honor and reverence due to God.

✡

It is a father's duty not only to provide for his minor children, but also to take care of their instruction, and to teach his son a trade and whatever is necessary for his future welfare.

Children's Obligations to Parents

"Respect your parents as you respect Me," says God.

✡

A son must, if necessary, feed and support his parents.

✡

A child owes his life to three: to God, to his father, and to his mother.

✡

Dama bar Netina, a heathen, of whom once some customers desired to buy wheat, for which they offered him a high price on account of its scarcity, said to them: "I cannot sell at present, for the key to the store lies under the pillow whereupon my father is now asleep. I dare not disturb his rest."

✡

Only when the father tempts the son to commit sin is disobedience justifiable.

✡

He who honors his father and mother enjoys the fruit in this life, and stores up a treasure for the future.

✡

While the son honors his parents, God holds it as if He were dwelling near the child, and were Himself receiving honor.

✡

Even if it happens that the son is a teacher, yet if the father is present, the son must rise before him in the presence of all his pupils.

When a son is called to do a service for his parents, he must first see that his person is tidy and clean; for a child must attend to his parents as though they were his king and queen.

✡

A child must not stand or sit in the place which his father is in the habit of occupying. He must not contradict his father, and when he names him he must use a term of respect, such as "my honored father."

✡

A child must love and honor his parents while they are living, and must love and respect them after they are dead; and as they loved and honored God, he must love and honor God, and thus make his parents live again in his own good deeds.

✡

If in after life the son prospers and is richer than his father, he must see that his prosperity is shared by his parents. He must not live in greater luxury than they; he must not allow them to suffer poverty while he enjoys wealth. But the son must not make himself obnoxious by too many attentions.

HONESTY

Do not buy stolen goods.

✡

An Israelite is prohibited from deceiving even an idolater.

✡

The most worthy crown is a good reputation.

✡

When the thief has no opportunity to steal he considers himself an honest man.

✡

It is not the amount of trade that makes the man poor or rich, but honest working and dealing.

He who unjustly hands over one man's goods to another, he shall pay God for it with his own soul.

✡

On the soul's appearance before the Divine Tribunal, the first question will be, "Hast thou been honest and faithful in all thy dealings?"

HONOR (NEIGHBOR'S)

Guard with jealous care thy neighbor's honor.

✡

Hold your neighbor's honor as sacred as your own.

✡

Be as eager to secure thy fellow's honor as thine own, and yield not easily to anger.

✡

The right way for man to choose is to do that which is honorable in his own eyes (i.e., approved by his conscience) and at the same time honorable in the eyes of his fellow men.

HOSPITALITY

Hospitality is as important as divine worship.

✡

Let thy house be open wide as a refuge, and let the poor be cordially received within thy walls.

HUMILITY

Rather be thou the tail among lions than the head among foxes.

He who humiliates himself will be lifted up; he who raises himself up will be humiliated.

✡

Whosoever runs after greatness, greatness runs away from him; he who runs from greatness, greatness follows him.

IDLENESS

When the woman slumbers, the work-basket falls to the ground.

IDOLATRY

"If your God hates idolatry, why does He not destroy it?" Rufus, the Roman, asked Rabbi Akiba. "Would you have Him destroy this beautiful world for the sake of the foolish people who worship the sun, the moon, or the stars, that are but the servants of God?" Akiba replied.

IMAGINATION, EVIL

The "Spirit of Evil" entices a man in this world, and testifies against him in the next.

✡

The "evil imagination" takes advantage only of visible objects.

✡

An evil eye, an "evil imagination," and misanthropy banish a man from the world.

IMMORTALITY

A special mansion will be given in Heaven to every pious man.

This world is like a road-side inn, but the world to come is like the real home.

✡

The longest life is insufficient for the fulfilment of half of man's desires.

✡

Better one hour's happiness in the next world than a whole lifetime of pleasure in this.

✡

One man may earn immortality by the work of a few short years, while others earn it by the work of a long life.

✡

He who lays up no store of good deeds during the working days of life can never enjoy the eternal Sabbath.

✡

This world is an antechamber to the next. Prepare thyself in the antechamber that thou mayest worthily enter the throne-room.

✡

The just of all nations have a portion in the future reward.

✡

For the righteous there is no rest, neither in this world nor in the next, for they go, say the Scriptures, "from strength unto strength, from task to task, until they shall see God in Zion."

✡

The grave is like a Melotian (silken) raiment for the pious man, who comes fully provided with provisions; the pious man can look upon the future life without fear, because he comes to the other world well prepared.

✡

"Man is born to die, but the dead shall live again." "Better is the day of death than the day of birth." These sayings are illustrated as follows: Two vessels sail on the ocean at one and the same time; the one is leaving, the other entering the harbor. For the one which arrived a number of friends had prepared a great feast, and with clapping of hands and great vociferations of joy, they celebrated her arrival, while the one which was leaving received sighs and tears. An intelligent man, who was a spectator of what passed, said: "Here quite the reverse appears to take place, as otherwise ought to happen. They rejoice over the one which cometh and feel saddened over the departure of the other. What a fallacy. Rejoice over the one which has accomplished its voyage and is returning from many dangers to safety, and bewail rather the vessel which is coming in, for she will have to brave again the storms of an inconstant sea." The same when man is born, great rejoicing takes place, while at his death much grief is expressed. One ought to weep at his birth, because no one is certain whether he will be able to overcome the dangers and temptations of life; whilst at his death one ought to feel pleased if he only leaves a good name behind him. At his birth man is entered into the book of death; when he dies he is entered into the book of life.

INGRATITUDE

Despise not small favors.

✡

Into the well from which thou drinkest do not cast a stone.

✡

He who eats and drinks, but blesses not the Lord, is even as he who stealeth.

✡

Once a man journeyed from Palestine to Babylon. While at his meal, he noticed a fierce strife between two birds, which ended in the apparent death of the one. When the other, however, noticed that its companion was dead, it hastened to search for a special kind of herb, which it brought and laid on the beak of the corpse, and soon thereafter the dead bird revived. The traveller saw this with astonishment and procured a sample of the herb. On journeying further, he met with a dead lion, and concluded to make the experiment upon him. He succeeded in reviving the lion, but no sooner had the latter regained his strength than he tore his benefactor to pieces.

When he was a puppy I fed him, and when he became a dog he bit me.

INTENTION

Do as much or little as thou canst, only let thy intention be always good.

ISRAEL

Every nation has its special guardian angel, its horoscopes, its ruling planets and stars. But there is no planet for Israel. Israel shall look but to God. There is no mediator between those who are called His children and their Father which is in Heaven.

JEALOUSY

He that cherishes jealousy in his heart, his bones rot.

✡

One seldom meets a man who likes his fellow artist.

JUDGING

Judge everybody favorably.

✡

Judge not thy neighbor until thou hast been placed in his position.

✡

Judge charitably every man and justify him all you can.

✡

Man sees the mote in his neighbor's eye, but knows not of the beam in his own.

A certain man who was once hired to work for a stipulated daily wage, and who worked for three years without having drawn his earnings, at length desired to go home and demanded his accumulations from his employer. "I have no money just now," said the employer. "Give me then some of your produce," demanded the employee. "I regret very much," said the master, "that I cannot comply with thy request." He asked him for cattle, for wine or vineyard, but the master declared he was unable to give him anything. With a heavy sigh the poor laborer took his tools and without a murmur departed. Scarcely had he gone when the employer ordered three asses laden with eatables, drinkables and wearing apparel, and personally rode to the residence of the laborer, who at once prepared a meal for his master, and they ate and drank together. After a while the employer drew forth a bag of money and handing it to the astonished employee, told him that the provisions-laden asses were his also. Thereupon the following dialogue ensued:

Employer. "What was in thy mind when I told thee I had no money?"

Employee. "I thought thou hadst unfortunately lost it."

Employer. "And when I told thee I had no cattle?"

Employee. "That others claimed it for a debt incurred prior to mine."

Employer. "What couldst thou have thought when I told thee I had no field?"

Employee. "That it might have been mortgaged."

Employer. "And when I told thee I had no fruit?"

Employee. "That it might not have been tithed yet."

Employer. "But what didst thou think when I told thee I had no vineyard nor wine?"

Employee. "It came to my mind that, perchance, thou hadst sanctified both wine and vineyard as gifts to the Temple."

Employer. "Ah, thou art a godly man. Faithfully hast thou complied with the ethical doctrine 'Judge everybody favorably.' Thou hast judged me favorably and God judge thee favorably."

JUDGMENT

God alone can judge.

In the hour when the Judge sits in judgment over his fellow men, he shall feel, as it were, a sword pointed at his own heart.

✡

When the soul appears before the Judgment-Seat it is asked:
"Hast thou been honest in all thy dealings?"
"Hast thou set aside a portion of thy time for the study of the Law?"
"Hast thou observed the first commandment?"
"Hast thou in trouble still hoped and believed in God?"
"Hast thou spoken the truth?"

JUSTICE

Whatever is hateful to thee, do not to thy neighbor.

✡

Thy neighbor's property must be as sacred to thee as thine own.

✡

From the very spoon that the carver carved, he has to swallow hot mustard.

✡

Wrong neither thy brother in faith nor him who differs from thee in faith.

✡

The shepherd is lame and the goats are nimble, but at the entrance of the fold they will have to meet him and at the door of the stable they will be counted.

LABOR

Love labor and hate to be a professional minister.

✡

Great is the dignity of labor; it honors man.

He who helps himself will be helped by God.

✡

The laborer is allowed to shorten his prayers.

✡

He who teaches his son no trade is as if he taught him to steal.

✡

The laborer at his work needs not rise before the greatest doctor.

✡

He who does not teach his son a handicraft trade neglects his parental duty.

✡

Beautiful is the intellectual occupation, if combined with some practical work.

✡

It is well to add a trade to your studies; you will then be free from sin.

✡

Work is more pleasant in the sight of the Lord than the merits of your fathers.

✡

He who lives by the work of his hands is greater than he who indulges in idle piety.

✡

He who derives his livelihood from the labor of his hands is as great as he who fears God.

✡

Happy the child who sees its parents engage in an honest trade; woe to the child who must blush on account of their dishonest trade.

✡

Get your living by skinning carcasses in the street, if you cannot otherwise, and do not say, "I am a priest, I am a great man; this work would not befit my dignity."

THE LAW

The beginning and end of the Law is kindness.

✡

The study of the Law, when not sustained by secular work, must come to an end, and involve one in sin.

✡

He who studies the Law in his youth gets its words absorbed in his blood, and they come readily from his mouth.

✡

He who studies the Law in his youth is like a young man marrying a virgin, suited to him; but he who begins the study of the Law in his old age is like an old man marrying a virgin who suits him, but who does not suit her.

LEVITY

Laughter and levity habituate a man to lewdness.

✡

Beware of too much laughter, for it deadens the mind and produces oblivion.

LIFE

Life is a passing shadow, says the Scripture. Is it the shadow of a tower or a tree? A shadow that prevails for a while? No; it is the shadow of a bird in his flight—away flies the bird and there is neither bird nor shadow.

LOANS

Lend to the poor in the time of their need.

Never take the clothes of wife or children in payment of a debt.

✡

If you have taken of a man his plough or his pillow for debt, return his plough in the morning and his pillow at night.

✡

The possessions of a widow, whether she be rich or poor, should not be taken in pawn.

LONG LIFE

"Wherewith prolongest thou life?" Rabbi Nechuma's disciples asked him once. And the master answered: "I never sought my honor at the expense of my associate's degradation, and the thought of a wrong done to me in daytime never went with me to bed at night."

LOVE

Love is blind.

✡

Love takes no advice.

✡

He who loves thee scolds thee.

✡

There is a compensation for everything except our first love.

✡

The love which shirks from reproving is no love.

✡

Three things produce love: culture of mind, modesty, and meekness.

✡

Love inspired by unworthy motives dies when those motives disappear.

When our conjugal love was strong, the width of the threshold offered sufficient accommodation for both of us; but now that it has cooled down, a couch sixty yards wide is too narrow.

MAN

Man, A Moral Being

The righteous control their desires, but the desires of the wicked control them.

Man's Free Will

Everything is foreordained by Heaven, except the fear of Heaven (i.e., the fear of God's anger when one is about to sin).

✡

Everything is ordained by God's providence, but freedom of choice is given to man.

✡

Whether a man be strong or weak, rich or poor, wise or foolish, depends mostly on circumstances that surround him from the time of his birth, but whether a man be good or bad, righteous or wicked, depends on his own free will.

God's Will, as The Guide of Man's Duties

Regulate thy will in accordance with God's will, and submit thy will to His will.

✡

Be bold as a leopard, light as an eagle, swift as a roe, and strong as a lion, to do the will of thy Father who is in heaven.

Man's Accountability to God

Every word, whether good or bad, accidental or intentional, is recorded in a book.

✡

Consider three things, and thou wilt never fall into sin: remember that there is above thee an All-Seeing Eye, an All-Hearing Ear, and a record of all thy actions.

✡

Consider three things and thou wilt never sin: remember whence thou comest, whither thou goest, and before whom thou wilt have to render an account for thy doings.

✡

What meaneth "Thou shalt love the Lord thy God with all thy soul"? It meaneth that thou must love Him, even if He demand thy soul.

✡

With the pious God is strict, even to a hair's breadth.

✡

Man is generally led the way which he is inclined to go.

✡

There is no death without individual sin, no pain without individual transgression. That same spirit that dictated in the Pentateuch*: 'And parents shall not die for their children, nor the children for their parents,' has ordained that no one should be punished for another's transgressions.

✡

Say not that sin and crime come from God or that He has caused thee to fall into sin, for He takes no pleasure in a sinful man. He hates every wickedness and abomination. He has created man from the beginning in purity and has left him to his free will to follow the path of righteousness or that of evil. Behold, fire and water have been put before thee, and thou mayest stretch out thy hand and choose, even as life and death are given thee to select; hail to him if he taketh life, but woe to him if he chooseth death.

✡

A king once engaged two watchmen to take care of his orchard. One was blind and the other lame. Still they answered the purpose very well; for their presence was quite sufficient to keep depredators at a distance. One evening the lame watchman was sitting in the orchard, when his eyes fell upon a bunch of luscious grapes, the first and only

Pentateuch] the first five books of the Bible.

ripe ones in the whole place. "Are you very thirsty?" said he to his blind companion, who was walking up and down, feeling his way with a stick. "Would you like a bunch of fine juicy grapes?" "Yes," was the blind man's reply. "But you know we cannot pick them. I am blind and cannot see. You are lame and cannot walk." "True," said the lame man. "Still we can get at them; take me on your back; I can guide you, and you can carry me to the grapes." And so they stole the precious fruit and ate it.

Now, the next day the king went into the orchard to gather this very cluster of grapes; for he had already observed it as being just fit for the table. It had vanished, and he at once taxed the watchmen with the theft.

"How can my lord, the king, accuse me of such a thing?" exclaimed the lame man. "Here I must sit all the days of my life, without moving a single inch; for am I not lame?"

"And how can my lord, the king, accuse me of such a thing, when I am blind?" asked the other. "How can the heart long after, or the hands reach, that which the eyes cannot behold?"

The king answered not a word. But he ordered his servants to place the lame man on the back of the blind man, and he condemned them to punishment just as if they had been one man. So it is with the soul and body of man. The soul cannot sin without the body, nor the body without the soul; the sin of both is the sin of each, and it will not avail in the great day of judgment to shirk the responsibility; but even as the lame and the blind watchmen, body and soul will be judged as one.

MEANS

The end does not justify the means.

THE MEDDLER

The meddler has his spoon in every pot.

MERCY

To deserve mercy, practise mercy.

The mercy we to others show, Heaven will show to us.

✡

He who judges without mercy will himself be judged.

✡

He who has compassion on his fellow man is accounted of the true seed of Abraham.

✡

Underneath the wings of the Seraphim are stretched the arms of divine mercy, ever ready to receive sinners.

THE MISER

A miser is as wicked as an idolater.

✡

The mice lie on his money bags.

✡

The birds in the air even despise the miser.

✡

Man is like that vegetation which sprouts from the ground as a tender plant, and gradually grows until at last it withers away and perisheth. This, O man, should teach thee to live pleasurably, enjoying the wealth that is thine while thou livest; for, consider, how long may that be? Life is brief, and death is sure. What matters it to thee if thy heirs will inherit a little more or a little less! Thou, O man, knowest not even how they will prize it, whether they will make good use of it or squander it.

MODERATION

Be moderate in all things.

✡

The horse fed too freely with oats oft becomes unruly.

Eat and drink to live; live not to eat and drink, for thus do the beasts.

✡

The sensible man drinks only when he is thirsty.

MODESTY

A good man is modest.

✡

They who are modest will not easily sin.

✡

Who are the pious? The modest. Who are the modest? Those who are bashful, knowing that God sees them.

MONEY

Money makes even bastards legitimate.

✡

He is rich who enjoys what he possesseth.

✡

He who lends money on usury consumes his own as well as the stranger's.

✡

Wealth may be like waters gathered in a house, which, finding no outlet, drown the owner.

✡

The fortune of this world is like a wheel with two buckets, the full becomes empty and the empty full.

✡

He who loves money cannot be righteous, and he who hastens after possessions is led away from the right path. Happy the rich whose hands are clean and who do not cling to possessions. If there be such a man, we will praise him as happy, for he has done much for his people. If thus tested and found unblemished, we will exalt him. If, having had the opportunity to deceive, he did it not, having had the means to act unjustly, he acted fairly.

OATHS

Which is a vain oath? If one affirms impossibilities; as, for instance, that a camel was flying in the air.

OBEDIENCE

Hasten to the performance of the slightest commandment, and flee from sin; for the performance of one virtuous act leads to another, and the commission of one sin leads to another; so is the reward of one virtuous act the performance of another, and the retribution of one sin the commission of another.

OBSCENITY

Let a man never allow an obscene word to pass out of his mouth.

OPPORTUNITY

If the thief has no opportunity, he thinks himself honorable.

ORPHANS

Money belonging to orphans should only be invested where the chance of gain is greater than the chance of loss.

PASSION

Who is strong? He who subdues his passion.

✡

The greater the man, the stronger his passion.

✡

Man's passions at first are like a cobweb's thread, at last become like thickest cord.

✡

Were it not for the existence of passions, no one would build a house, marry a wife, beget children, or do any work.

✡

The wicked is in the power of his passion; the righteous keeps passion in his power.

✡

What should man do in order to live? Deaden his passions. What should man do in order to die? Give himself entirely to life.

✡

First, our passions are like travellers, making a brief stay, then like guests visiting us day by day, until at last they become our masters, holding us beneath their sway.

PATRIOTISM

Do not isolate thyself from the community and its interests.

✡

Were it not for patriotism, sterile lands would be deserted.

✡

It is sinful to deceive the government regarding taxes and duties.

✡

Do not aspire for public offices; but where there are no men, try thou to be a man.

He who revolts against the government commits as great a sin as if he revolted against God.

✡

Those who work for the community shall work without selfishness, but with the pure intention to promote its welfare.

✡

Pray for the welfare of the government, since if it were not for the awe which it inspires, men would swallow each other alive.

PEACEFULNESS

The Bible was given to establish peace.

✡

Be the first to hold out the hand of peace.

✡

Where there is no peace, nothing flourishes.

✡

Be a disciple of Aaron, loving peace, and pursuing peace.

✡

What is sweeter than sweetness? Peace after enmity.

✡

Sow peace at home, scatter its fruits abroad.

✡

Peace is the wisp of straw which binds the sheaf of blessings.

✡

He who maketh peace among strivers will inherit eternal life.

✡

Discord is like a leak in a cistern. Drop by drop all the water escapes.

✡

When two men quarrel, he who is first silent is the better man.

Great is peace, for it is to the world what yeast is to the dough.

✡

Man, be ever soft and pliable like a reed, and not hard and unbending like a cedar.

✡

When do justice and good will meet? When the contending parties are made to agree peaceably.

✡

Peace is the vessel in which all God's blessings are preserved to us and preserved by us.

✡

Strife is like a jet of water pouring through a crevice; the wider the crevice, the stronger the flow.

✡

Those who, when offended, do not give offence, when hearing slighting remarks, do not retaliate, they are the friends of God, they shall shine forth like the sun in its glory.

✡

Have a soft reply to turn away anger, and let thy peace be abundant with thy brother, with thy friend, and with everybody, even with the Gentile in the street, that thou shalt be beloved above and esteemed below.

PERDITION

Envy, lust, ambition, bring a man to perdition.

PERJURY

The sin of perjury is great.

God may delay all other punishments, but the sin of perjury is avenged straightway.

✡

Do not accustom yourself to use oaths, or you will be led into perjury.

PERSECUTION

Be of them that are persecuted, not of them that persecute.

✡

Whosoever does not persecute them that persecute him, whosoever takes an offence in silence, he who does good because of love, he who is cheerful under his sufferings—they are the friends of God, and of them the Scripture says: "They shall shine forth as does the sun at noonday."

✡

There is not a single bird more persecuted than the dove; yet God has chosen her to be offered up on the altar. The bull is hunted by the lion, the sheep by the wolf, the goat by the tiger. And God said: "Bring me a sacrifice, not from them that persecute, but from them that are persecuted."

PERSEVERANCE

If thou hast commenced a good action, leave it not incomplete.

PHYSICIANS

Wait not to honor the physician till thou fallest sick.

✡

Medicine is a science whose practise is authorized by God Himself.

We ought not to live in a town where no physician resides.

✡

The strict observance of Sabbath and the Day of Atonement is set aside, when the physician declares such desecration necessary, even against the will of the patient.

✡

God causes the remedial herbs to grow up from the ground; they become a healing cause in the hands of the physicians, and from them the druggist prepares the remedies.

POPULAR PREJUDICE

The serpent's tail had a long time followed the directions of the head with the best results. One day the tail began, "Thou appearest always foremost, but I must remain in the background. Why should I not also sometimes lead?" "Well," replied the head, "thou shalt have thy will for once." The tail, rejoiced, accordingly took the lead. Its first exploit was to drag the body into a miry ditch. Hardly escaped from that unpleasant situation, it crept into a fiery furnace; and when relieved from there, it got entangled among briers and thorns. What caused all these misfortunes? Because the head submitted to be guided by the tail. When the lower classes are guided by the higher, all goes well, but if the higher orders suffer themselves to be swayed by popular prejudices, they all suffer together.

POSITION

No position can dignify the man. It is the man who dignifies the position.

POVERTY

The Eternal is the advocate of the poor.

Healthy poverty is opulence, compared with ailing wealth.

✡

Be mindful of the children of the poor, for learning comes from them.

PRAYER

Cleanse your heart before praying.

✡

Always pray with humility and with a clear conscience.

✡

Prayer without devotion is like a body without life.

✡

Better little prayer with devotion than much without devotion.

✡

Blessed are the women who send their children to the house of prayer.

✡

Even when the gates of heaven are shut to prayer, they are open to those of tears.

✡

The value of the words uttered with the lips is determined by the devotion of the heart.

✡

To pray loudly is not a necessity of devotion; when we pray we must direct our hearts towards heaven.

✡

Look not on thy prayers as on a task; let the supplication be sincere.

✡

Prayer is Israel's only weapon, a weapon inherited from its fathers, a weapon tried in a thousand battles.

PRIDE

Pride is like idolatry.

✡

A penny in an empty box rattles loudly.

✡

The prayers of the proud are never heard.

✡

Pride leads to the destruction of man.

✡

Pride is a sign of the worst poverty—ignorance.

✡

Even to his own household the overbearing is distasteful.

✡

The proud man is troubled at the slightest wind.

✡

The proud are pettish* and the pettish are foolish.

✡

He who hardens his heart with pride softens his brain with the same.

✡

The Messiah will not come until haughtiness shall have ceased among men.

✡

It requires but the slightest breeze of ill-luck to cast down the proud, and quite right, too; for the immense ocean, which consists of countless drops of water, is nevertheless disturbed by the slightest breeze; and will there be anything more necessary to humble men, in whose veins only one drop of blood is flowing?

**pettish*] peevish.

PROMISES

Good men promise little and perform much.

✡

Wicked men promise much and perform nothing.

PUBLIC OPINION

Despise not public opinion.

✡

The voice of the people is as the voice of God.

✡

Not what you say about yourself, but what others say.

✡

He who fears the opinion of the world more than his own conscience has but little self-respect.

✡

Whosoever is loved by mankind is also loved by the Supreme, but whosoever is not loved by mankind is not loved by the Supreme.

✡

If one person tell thee that thou hast asses' ears, do not mind it; but if two persons make this assertion, at once place a pack-saddle upon thy back.

PURPOSE

Every union for a divine purpose is destined to last.

QUARRELING

Quarreling is the weapon of the weak.

RELIGION

Religion maketh the man.

✡

Religion is the light of the world.

✡

Without religion there can be no true morality.

✡

God's commandments are intended to enhance the value and enjoyment of life, but not to mar it and make it gloomy.

✡

He who devotes himself to the mere study of religion without engaging in works of love and mercy is like one who has no God.

REPENTANCE

When a man has turned away from sin, reproach him no more.

✡

Happy the man who repents in the strength of his manhood.

✡

One contrition in man's heart is better than many flagellations.

✡

The aim and end of all wisdom are repentance and good works.

✡

As the ocean never freezes, so the gates of repentance never close.

✡

So great is the virtue of repentance that it prolongs a man's years.

✡

The tears of true penitence are not shed in vain.

He who repeatedly sins, looking forward to penitence to cover his sins, his penitence will avail him nothing.

✡

Even the most righteous shall not attain to so high a place in heaven as the truly repentant.

✡

One hour employed in this world in the exercise of repentance and good deeds is preferable to a whole life in the world to come; and one hour's refreshment of spirit in the future world is preferable to the entire life in this.

✡

The Day of Atonement is given for the expiation of sins committed against God; but the Day of Atonement will not expiate sins committed against a fellow man, unless the offender has asked pardon of the offended.

✡

In three ways may we repent: by publicly confessing our sins, by manifesting sorrow for sins committed, and by good deeds, which are as sacrifices before the Lord.

✡

Repent one day before thy death. There was a king who bade all his servants to a great repast, but did not indicate the hour; some went home and put on their best garments and stood at the door of the palace, others said, "There is ample time, the king will let us know beforehand." But the king summoned them of a sudden, and those that came in the best garments were well received, but the foolish ones who came in their slovenliness were turned away in disgrace. Repent to-day lest to-morrow ye might be summoned.

✡

And it came to pass that a great ship, while sailing upon the ocean, was driven from its course by a high wind and finally was becalmed close to a pleasant-appearing island, where they dropped anchor. There grew upon this island beautiful flowers and luscious fruits in great profusion, and tall trees lent a cooling shade to the place, that appeared to the ship's passengers most desirable and inviting. They divided themselves into five parties; the first party determined not to leave the ship, for said they, "A fair wind may arise, the anchor may be raised, and the ship sail on, leaving us behind: we will not risk the chance of missing our destination for the temporary pleasure which this island offers." The second party went on shore for a short time, enjoyed the perfume of the flowers, tasted the fruits, and returned to the ship happy and refreshed, finding their places as they had left them; losing nothing, but rather gaining in health and spirits by the recreation of their visit on shore. The third party also visited the island, but they tarried on the way. Meanwhile a fair wind arose, seeing which they hurried to the ship and arrived just as the sailors were lifting the anchor. Many of them lost their places, and were not as comfortable during the balance of their voyage as at the outset. They were wiser, however, than the fourth party, which stayed so long on the island, and tasted so deeply of its pleasures that they minded neither the wind nor the ship's bell that called them. Said they: "The sails are still to be set; we may enjoy ourselves a few minutes more." Again the bell sounded, and still they lingered, thinking, "The captain will not sail without us." So they remained until they saw the ship moving; then in wild haste they swam after it and scrambled up the sides, but the bruises and injuries which they encountered in so doing were not healed during the remainder of the voyage. But, alas for the fifth party. They ate and drank so deeply that they did not even hear the bell, and when the ship started they were left behind. Then the wild beasts hid in the thickets made them a prey, and they who escaped this evil perished from the poison of surfeit.

The "ship" is our good deeds, which bear us to our destination, heaven. The "island" typifies the pleasures of the world, which the first set of passengers refused to taste or look upon, but which when enjoyed temperately as by the second party, make our lives pleasant, without causing us to neglect our duties. These pleasures must not be allowed, however, to gain too strong a hold upon our senses. True, we may return, as the third party, while there is yet time and with but little bad effect, or even as the fourth party at the eleventh hour, be saved, but with many bruises and injuries which cannot be entirely healed; but we are in danger of becoming as the last party, spending a lifetime in the pursuit of vanity, forgetting the future, and perishing even of the poison concealed in the sweets which attract us.

REPROOF

He who cannot bear one word of reproof will have to hear many.

RESIGNATION

Blessed is he who meekly bears his trials, of which everyone has his share.

✡

When misfortune befalls you examine your conduct and acknowledge that God's chastisement is just.

✡

During Rabbi Meir's absence from home two of his sons died. Their mother, hiding her grief, awaited the father's return, and then said to him: "My husband, some time since two jewels of inestimable value were placed with me for safe keeping. He who left them with me called for them to-day, and I delivered them into his hands." "That is right," said the Rabbi, approvingly. "We must always return cheerfully and faithfully all that is left in our care." Shortly after this the Rabbi asked for his sons, and the mother, taking him by the hand, led him gently to the chamber of death. Meir gazed upon his sons, and realizing the truth, wept bitterly. "Weep not, beloved husband," said his noble wife; "didst thou not say to me we must return cheerfully, when 'tis called for, all that has been placed in our care? God gave us these jewels, he left them with us for a time, and we gloried in their possession; but now that he calls for his own, we should not repine."

✡

Rabbi Judah said: "If a person weeps and mourns excessively for a lost relative, his grief becomes a murmur against the will of God, and he may soon be obliged to weep for another death. We should justify the decree of God, and exclaim with Job, 'The Lord gave and the Lord hath taken; blessed be the name of the Lord.'"

REVENGE

Misery and remorse are the children of revenge.

✡

He who gratifies revenge destroys his own house.

✡

Rabbi Meir was vociferous against evil doers and often prayed God, saying, “Destroy the sinners.” Beruriah, his pious wife, gently admonished him, saying, “Rather pray that God destroy sin and the sinners will be no more.”

REWARDS

In proportion to thy efforts will be thy recompense.

✡

The reward of good works is like dates; sweet and ripening late.

✡

The measure man metes to man the same will be meted to him.

✡

Be not like servants who wait on their master expecting to receive reward, but be you like those who serve their master without expecting reward.

THE RIGHTEOUS

The righteous are even greater in death than in life.

✡

When the righteous die, they live; for their example lives.

✡

The loss of a pious man is a loss to his whole generation.

✡

The righteous promise little and do much.

✡

The righteous are heard when they persevere in prayer.

✡

The righteous need no monuments. Their deeds are their monuments.

Alexander one day wandered to the gates of paradise and knocked. The guardian angel asked: "Who is there?" "I, Alexander." "Who is Alexander?" "Alexander, the conqueror of the world." "We know him not. He cannot enter here. This is the Lord's gate; only the righteous enter here."

✡

The death of the righteous is a calamity equal in magnitude to the burning of the Temple.

ROBBERY

Buy nothing from a thief.

✡

The thief's end is the gallows.

✡

It is wrong to receive a present from a thief.

✡

The receiver is as bad as the thief.

✡

If one finds a marked article he should advertise it publicly, so that the owner may recover it.

SABBATH

The Sabbath is given to man, not man to the Sabbath.

SECRETS

Do not reveal thy secret to the apes.

✡

Thy secret is thy slave. If thou let it loose, thou becomest its slave.

Though thousands do thy friendship seek,
To one alone thy secret speak.

✡

Keep shut the doors of thy mouth
Even from the wife of thy bosom.

✡

That which man conceals in his innermost chamber is plain and manifest to God.

SELF-RESPECT

He who is ashamed will not easily commit sin.

✡

There is a great difference between him who is ashamed before his own self and him who is only ashamed before others.

✡

There is hope for a man who is capable of being ashamed.

✡

He who is bashful before others but is not before himself is wanting in self-respect.

SELF-SUPPORT

A person dependent on the table of another has the world darkened.

✡

A man should be opposed to taking alms as well as to being a burden on the community.

✡

It is better to be a menial than to live upon the charity of others.

✡

All I weighed on scales, but found nothing lighter than bran; lighter than bran, however, is a son-in-law living in his father-in-law's house: lighter still, a guest introduced by another guest.

✡

Whoever has no possessions may be compared to an infant that has lost its mother. It may be nourished by many women, but it does not thrive, because a mother's love no one is able to supply. The man who is supported by others, were it even by his own father or mother, or his children, never feels that contentment which his own exertions would give him.

SICK

It is a bounden duty to visit the sick.

✡

If your neighbor is sick, pray for him.

SILENCE

Silence is consent.

✡

If silence is becoming to a wise man, how much more so to a fool?

✡

Do not deem thy speech secure, for the wall has ears.

✡

If a word spoken in time is worth one piece of money, silence in its time is certainly worth two.

SIN

Sin begets sin.

Curse the sin, not the sinner.

✡

Commit a sin twice, and you will think it perfectly allowable.

✡

The wiser the man, the more careful should he be of his conduct.

✡

To resist sin is as meritorious as to be actively engaged in a good work.

✡

A man commits sin in secret; but the Holy One proclaims it openly.

SINCERITY

Be always sincere in your yea and your nay.

SLANDER

To slander is to murder.

✡

Teach thy tongue to say, "I do not know."

✡

Better no ear at all than one that listeneth to evil.

✡

Guard thy mouth from uttering an unseemly word.

✡

Rather be thrown into a fiery furnace than bring anyone to public shame.

✡

Four shall not enter Paradise; the scoffer, the liar, the hypocrite, and the slanderer.

A man's merits should be fully stated in his absence, but only partially in his presence.

✡

A slanderer injures three persons: himself, him that receives the slander and the slandered person.

✡

Listen, sir, to my words, and give ear to my utterances. Keep from strifes with thy neighbor, and if thou seest that thy friend does anything wrong, guard thy tongue from gossip.

✡

R. Gamaliel ordered his servant Tobi to bring something good from the market, and he brought a tongue. At another time he told him to bring something bad, and he also returned with a tongue. "Why did you on both occasions fetch a tongue?" the Rabbi asked. "It is the source of good and evil," Tobi replied, "if it is good there is nothing better, if it is bad there is nothing worse."

✡

A king, who was dangerously sick, was recommended to drink the milk of a lioness. The king offered a high price for it, and a man tendered his services to procure it. After many dangerous exploits the man succeeded in procuring it, and hastened to bring the milk to the court. While on his journey he stopped at a tavern; the different members of his body engaged in a lively dispute. The feet commenced to assert, "If we had not carried the other members, you had never succeeded in procuring the milk!" "What an arrogance!" the hands exclaimed. "If we had not milked the lioness, your running would have been of little benefit." The eyes said, "Had we not shown you the way, and the lioness, what had you been without us?" The heart said, "It was my direction that secured the success!" At last the tongue participated in the dispute: "What would all your actions amount to without me?" The other members merely laughed derisively at the claims of the tongue, which, angry at such treatment, said, "You shall find it out to your sorrow." When the man arrived at the court and offered the milk, the tongue called out, "That is milk from a Kalba (bitch)." The king became very wroth and ordered the man to be hung. Now all the members trembled, while the tongue laughed. "Did I not tell you that you are given into my power? But I will save you again. Bring me back before the king!" the tongue cried, and when again in the presence of the king it said, "You misunderstood the meaning of my words. I brought milk of a Lebia (lioness), only in my haste I used the Arabic term for lioness, Kalba." The milk being examined and found to be as the man said, he was richly rewarded. The tongue then proudly exclaimed, "Life and death are given into my power!"

SLAVES

Slaves should never be addressed as such, for the name itself is contemptible.

SOLDIERS

The soldiers fight and the kings are called heroes.

THE SOUL

The soul of one good man is worth as much as all the earth.

✡

Hillel, the gentle, the beloved sage,
Expounded day by day the sacred page
To his disciples in the house of learning;
And day by day, when home at eve returning,
They lingered, clust'ring round him, loath to part
From him whose gentle rule won every heart.
But evermore, when they were wont to plead
For longer converse, forth he went with speed,
Saying each day: "I go—the hour is late—
To tend the guest who doth my coming wait,"
Until at last they said: "The Rabbi jests
When telling us thus of his daily guests
That wait for him." The Rabbi paused awhile,
Then made answer: "Think you I beguile
You with an idle tale? Not so forsooth!
I have a guest, whom I must tend in truth.

Is not the soul of man indeed a guest,
Who in this body deigns awhile to rest,
And dwells with me all peacefully to-day;
To-morrow—may it not have fled away?"

✡

"Let thy garments be always white."—Eccl. ix. 8.

A king once distributed state robes among his servants. The wiser among them took great care of these gifts; not a single spot sullied their purity, not a single stain dimmed their brilliancy. But the foolish servants did all their work arrayed in these robes, forgetting the grandeur of the gift, and the dignity of the donor.

Suddenly the king ordered the robes to be returned unto him. The wise servants came and restored the dresses spotless and undefiled, but the foolish ones brought theirs bedaubed and spoilt.

The king was rejoiced at the thoughtful conduct of the wise servants, but was incensed at the carelessness of the others.

"Throw them into prison," he exclaimed; "let them there cleanse their garments. But the good and discreet shall remain about me, and glory in their splendor, for they are worthy thereof."

Such is the way of God: he giveth to all alike a precious gift, a pure and spotless soul. The pious who make good use of this divine gift are permitted to enjoy eternal bliss, but the wicked are debarred from this happiness, till their souls are purified from the taints of sin.

SPEECH

Speech is the messenger of the heart.

SWEARING

Swear not, even to the truth, unless the court compels you to do so.

✡

The world trembled with dread when God exclaimed: "Take not my name in vain."

SYMPATHY

Man's thoughts and ways shall always be in contact and sympathy with his fellow men.

✡

To what is a man likened, who consoles with his neighbor twelve months after his bereavement by death? He is like a surgeon, asking a man who had once broken his leg to let him break it again and heal it, that he may show him what excellent skills he has.

TEMPER

One who restrains his temper, all his sins meet forgiveness.

TEMPERAMENT

There are four kinds of temperament: To be easily provoked, and to be easily pacified, is to neutralize a bad quality with a good one; to be provoked with difficulty, and to be pacified with difficulty, is to neutralize a good quality by a bad one; to be provoked with difficulty, and to be easily pacified, is the temperament of a holy man; to be easily provoked and pacified with difficulty is the temperament of a wicked man.

TEMPTATION

Happy the man who resists his temptations.

✡

The study of God's Word is the only antidote against temptation.

THOUGHTS

Sinful thoughts are even more dangerous than sin itself.

TOLERANCE

Support the aged without reference to religion; respect the learned without reference to age.

✡

The virtuous of all nations participate in eternal bliss.

✡

The Lord who proclaimed the Law of Sinai is the God of all nations.

✡

"Before me," said the Lord, "there is no difference between Jew and Gentile; he that accomplishes good, will I reward accordingly."

✡

When Abraham left Ur in Chaldea, he settled near Bethel, for the pasturage was good, the country well watered, with a very scanty population, at which he rejoiced, as his flocks could graze unmolested. But Sarah lamented their late pleasant home, on the plain, Moreb, and their friendly neighbors. Being tired of their solitude, she begged her husband to invite any wayfarers to their tent to partake of their hospitality. One day Abraham noticed an old man riding as one in haste, and, inquiring of him the cause, discovered the man to be in search of a scattered herd of cattle, so he invited him to his tent to refresh himself, promising that some of his young men would assist in the search. The old man assented. Abraham had a bath prepared and a goodly feast, prior to the eating of which Abraham invoked a blessing from God, in which the old man refused to join. On being asked the reason for his impiety he acknowledged being a fire worshipper. Abraham, full of indignation at his refusal to join in prayer, drove the travel-worn old man out of his tent. As he departed sorrowfully an angel of the Lord appeared to Abraham and asked him what he did, saying: "See you not that the Lord has had patience with this ignorant man these seventy years—can you not dwell with him for an hour?"

So Abraham recalled the old man, urged him to partake, made ready his young men, who soon returned with the missing cattle, and who assisted the traveller to drive them home; on which the old man, in leaving, blessed Abraham and Sarah, and said their kindly actions made a believer of him, and that a living fire was burning in his heart to be of service to his fellow man.

TRIAL

The future gains from present pains.

✡

Blessed be he who bears his trials. Everyone has his share.

✡

He who cheerfully submits to sufferings brings salvation to the world.

TRUTH

Truth is the seal of God.

✡

Promise little and do much.

✡

Truth is its own witness.

✡

Truth tells its own tale.

✡

The liar is worse than the thief.

✡

Always acknowledge the truth.

✡

Truth will stand, but falsehood must fall.

✡

Truth is the seal to God's works.

✡

Truth is heavy, therefore few carry it.

✡

Truth lasts forever, but falsehood must vanish.

Deception in words is a greater sin than deception in money matters.

✡

To be faithless to a given promise is as sinful as idolatry.

✡

This is the punishment of the liar, that when he tells the truth nobody believes him.

✡

It is sinful to deceive any man, be he even a heathen.

✡

To break a verbal engagement, though legally not binding, is a moral wrong.

UPSTARTS

When the castle goes to ruin, castle is still its name; when the dunghill rises, still it is a dunghill.

USEFULNESS

In all God's creation there is not a single object without a purpose.

✡

Use thy best vase to-day, for to-morrow it may, perchance, be broken.

USURY

No Israelite is allowed to lend usuriously to a non-Israelite.

✡

The practise of usury is as wicked as the shedding of blood.

The possessions of him who lends usuriously shall sooner or later decrease and vanish.

✡

The testimony of a usurer is not valid before the court of Justice.

✡

The usurer will have no share in an everlasting life.

✡

The usurer will not prosper.

VOW

He who makes a solemn vow without fulfilling it, his book will be searched.

WINE

Drink not, and you will not sin.

✡

When the wine enters, the secret goes out.

✡

When Satan cannot come himself, he sends wine as a messenger.

WISDOM

A scholar is greater than a prophet.

✡

Study is more meritorious than sacrifice.

✡

Let thy house be a resort of the wise.

Who is a wise man? He who learns of all men.

✡

Who is a wise man? He who looks into the future.

✡

The disciples of the wise are engaged all their days in building up the world.

✡

The end of wisdom is repentance and good works.

✡

Wisdom is a tree and active virtue is its fruit.

✡

The world depends on its school-children.

✡

For the blind in mind there is no physician.

✡

A town which has no school should be abolished.

✡

Learn a little here and a little there, and you will increase in knowledge.

✡

An old man (i.e., one entitled to veneration) is only he who has acquired wisdom.

✡

If a man has knowledge, he has all things; if he has no knowledge, he has nothing.

✡

Culture in a woman is better than gold.

✡

Culture of heart is better than culture of learning.

Jerusalem was destroyed because the instruction of the young was neglected.

✡

The world is only saved by the breath of the school-children.

✡

Even for the rebuilding of the Temple the instruction of the children must not be interrupted.

✡

The chief thing is not learning, but the deed.

✡

Beware of an over-pious ignoramus and of one badly trained.

✡

If a man does not go after wisdom, wisdom will not come to him.

✡

Learn first and philosophize afterwards.

✡

Whosoever tries to make gain by the crown of learning perishes.

✡

The more knowledge, the more spiritual life.

✡

Wisdom increases with years; and so does folly.

✡

Knowledge without religion blesses not its possessor.

✡

The teachers are the guardians of a State.

✡

"Repeat," "repeat," that is the best medicine for memory.

✡

He who instructs a child is as if he had created it.

The rivalry of scholars advances learning.

✡

God looks to the heart of man and then to the mind.

✡

One learned, who is not inwardly as outwardly, is not to be looked upon as learned.

✡

Honor the sons of the poor; it is they who bring science into splendor.

✡

The Lord is not with him who, while possessing great knowledge, has no sense of duty.

✡

If you have not desired wisdom in your youth, how will you acquire her in your old age?

✡

If you interrupt your studies for one day, it will take you two to regain what you have lost.

✡

Do not be wise in words alone, but also in deeds, for the wisdom of deeds will be necessary for the world to come, while the wisdom of words remains on earth.

✡

The ultimate end of all knowledge and wisdom is man's inner purification and the performance of good and noble deeds.

✡

Ignorance and conceit go hand in hand.

✡

Without knowledge there can be neither true morality nor piety.

✡

Be eager to acquire knowledge; it does not come to thee by inheritance.

Teach the children of the poor without compensation, and do not favor the children of the rich.

✡

If thou hast acquired knowledge, what canst thou lack? If thou lackest knowledge, what canst thou acquire?

✡

It is necessary to have a knowledge of the world, besides a knowledge of the Holy Law.

✡

He who acquires knowledge, without imparting it to others, is like a myrtle in the desert, where there is no one to enjoy it.

✡

Who are you whose prayers alone have prevailed? I am a teacher of little children.

✡

He who has the least understanding has the most questions.

✡

To what may he be compared who teaches a child? To one who writes on clean paper; and to what may he be compared who teaches an old man? To one who writes on blotted paper.

✡

To what may he be compared who learns from children? To one who eats sour grapes and drinks wine just from the press; and to what may he be compared who learns from the aged? To one who eats ripe grapes and drinks old wine.

✡

He who has more learning than good works is like a tree with many branches but few roots, which the first wind throws on its face; whilst he whose works are greater than his knowledge is like a tree with many roots and fewer branches, but which all the winds of heaven cannot uproot.

✡

Be wise, my son, be prescient, acquire truth and esteem uprightness.

Look upon fools as empty shadows. Avoid the advice of the ignorant; build when he advises to tear down, and attach yourself to the wise.

✡

You should revere the teacher even more than the father. The latter only brought you into the world, the former indicates the way into the next. But blessed is the son who has learned from his father; he shall revere him both as his father and his master; and blessed is the father who has instructed his son.

✡

If any one telleth thee he has searched for knowledge and not attained it, believe him not; if he telleth thee he has attained knowledge without searching for it, believe him not; but if he telleth thee that he has searched for knowledge and attained it, thou mayest believe him.

✡

Four dispositions are found among those who sit for instruction before the wise, and they may be respectively compared to a sponge, a funnel, a strainer, and a sieve; the sponge imbibes all; the funnel receives at one end and discharges at the other; the strainer suffers the wine to pass through, but retains the lees*; and the sieve removes the bran, but retains the fine flour.

WOMAN

A woman loves a poor youth rather than a rich old man.

✡

A woman schemes while plying the spindle.

✡

A woman is a shrewder observer of guests than a man.

✡

A woman is more desirous of entering the state of matrimony than a man.

---

*_lees_] dregs.

A woman prefers poverty with the affection of her husband to riches without it.

✡

The Emperor Hadrian is introduced as conversing with Rabbi Gamaliel on several religious questions, with the object of casting ridicule on the Bible. Hadrian exclaims: "Why, your God is represented therein as a thief. He surprised Adam in his sleep and robbed him of one of his ribs." The Rabbi's daughter, who is present, craves permission to reply to the Emperor. This is granted. "But first let me implore thy imperial protection, puissant sire," she exclaims. "A grave outrage has been perpetrated upon our house. Under the cover of night an audacious thief broke into our house and took a silver flagon from our chest of plate and left a golden one in its stead." "What a welcome thief," cried Hadrian. "Would that such robbers might visit my palace every day." "And was not the Creator such a thief as this?" archly rejoins the blushing damsel—"Who deprived Adam of a rib and in lieu thereof gave him a loving, lovely bride?"

YOUTH

Happy is he who fears God when in the prime of life.

✡

Some are old in their youth, others young in their old age.

✡

Youth is a crown of roses, old age is a crown of rosemary.

✡

Alas! for one thing that goes and never returns. What is it? Youth.